Pour R

Choices

Every Sip Tells a Story

Beyond the Glass

Renee Ventrice

Pour Relationship Choices: Every Sip Tells a Story Beyond the Glass Copyright © 2025 by Renee Ventrice.

All rights reserved, including the right to reproduce this book or portions thereof in any form whatsoever. For permission requests, contact publisher details below.

For event or media inquiries, including author appearances, speaking engagements, special discounts for bulk book orders, or to schedule an event, contact: media@weldwoodpublishing.com

ISBN: 978-1-968182-00-7 (paperback)
ISBN: 978-1-968182-01-4 (digital ebook)

This book is intended for informational and entertainment purposes only. Readers should consult appropriate professionals for personal, legal, medical, or psychological matters. The author and publisher disclaim any liability arising directly or indirectly and are not responsible for any consequences resulting from the use or misuse of this book or any information contained herein.

While this book is based on real-life experiences and observations, some names, identifying characteristics, and details may have been changed to protect privacy.

Published by:

Weldwood Publishing
38345 River Dr Lebanon, OR 97355
admin@weldwoodpublishing.com | (907) 953-9167
https://weldwoodpublishing.com/

Limited Edition Advanced Copy: Printed in the USA

TABLE OF CONTENTS

Foreword 5
Note From The Author...........................7
Part I: The Dump Bucket..........................9
    My Toxic Ex   11
    Feaux-Gettabout-It…   16
    Fear Is a Factor   22
    Blinded By The Light   30
Part II: Wine Fridge 37
    Business Blends Beyond Friends 39
    Lost In Translation   45
    Booty Call   51
Part III: Wine Cellar 55
    Love at First Sip   57
    Ride Or Die   64
    Why You So Salty?   69
    S-motherly Love   77
    Puzzles & The Patriarch   82
    Paws On My Heart   89
    Raising a Chardonnay Kid in a 97
    Pinot Noir World   97
    From Planted to Priceless 102
Glossary 118
Meet Renee… 120

Foreword

As the older (and admittedly more conservative) sister, I've often found myself marveling at my sister's fearless spirit. She is adventurous, whimsical, and never afraid to explore the edges - whether in business, in life, or, as this book reveals, in our "people lessons".

I don't drink wine, but I do understand that the stories we tell ourselves - and each other - about relationships are often best understood when we let them breathe, swirl them around a little, and look honestly at what they reveal.

Renee has chosen to share personal moments and reflections that invite each of us to examine the quality of our own relationships. Her transparency is a gift - one that encourages us to live with greater courage, honesty, and openness.

In these pages, my sister has artfully uncorked the truth about connection, heartbreak, joy, and growth through the lens of wine characteristics. It's insightful, brave, sometimes hilarious, and always deeply human. I may not share her taste for Merlot or Malbec, but I do share her reverence for the lessons at the bottom of the glass.

It is an honor to be included in this beautiful expression of who she is, and I cherish her for the wild, wise, and wonderful soul she continues to be.

- Forever proud to call you my sister, lovingly, Patrice!

Note From The Author

Dear Reader,

Thank you for being here. In today's world, everyone is fighting for your attention and I am truly honored you spent time with me & my book. I hope reading it was as fun for you as writing it has been for me!

You know how a wine tasting is a few ounces of each wine so you can decide whether or not you want to buy a bottle, or join the club...?

Think of POUR Relationship Choices as a tasting: each chapter is a sample, journaling in the book is buying the bottle, sharing it with others is joining the club.

I am so excited to learn where you saw yourself within these pages and how you uncorked your own POURsonality as we explored wine through different perspectives, and reflected on past relationships in a new light.

There is even more to discover in the Vintage Collector's edition! You'll find bonus chapters (including two pivotal relationships I'm still struggling to put into words) and deeper wine geekery along with wine collector tools and resources. Think of that version as the barrel tasting of all the library wines!

Cheers to you for sipping along with me as We Get Though This Thing Called Life. I tip my Raspberry Beret to each of you in thanks for allowing me to be your Lady Cab Driver.

While some chapters may cause Controversy, there is something to Adore about every Strange Relationship, especially the Beautiful Ones. And now, Let's Go Crazy. (IYKYK)

Scan the code to answer a few questions, share your feedback & to help make future books in this series an even stronger reflection of your POUR Relationship Choices.

Cheers Y'all!

- Renee 🖤

Part I: The Dump Bucket

Some POUR Choices are LITERALLY POOR Choices.

But they help us to grow, improve and have great stories to tell at dinner parties. Based in truth, then embellished in imagination, these are experiences that shaped better decisions as I poured my way through life.

From walks of shame to hilarious hiccups- when your POURsonality pops up here, you'll know it.

Chapter 1
My Toxic Ex

We went through some rough nights together. We knew we weren't good for each other, yet night after night we got together, and at dawn, I realized I'd made the same mistake again.

Sure, I would make it four, even five days without you, vowing each Sunday morning that *this* Saturday was our last rendezvous - I meant it every time. But come Friday night, I found myself excitedly slipping into our old routine. It felt so good to hold you. I'd pull my comfortable, college hoodie over my head - you remember, the one I was wearing the night we met?

Back then, we'd snuggle into the couch and binge on bad TV, worse microwaved snacks, and then... I'd wake up angry that you'd dragged me into another all-nighter that left me sick with guilt and completely exhausted - while you carried on without looking back at the mess. Me. *I* was the mess you left behind.

The next weekend, I went back for more, even though I knew it wouldn't end well. It never *did* with us. We always started with long, hard laughter as we pieced together shenanigans that straddled the thin line between having fun and committing a felony. Yes, those were nights made of reckless dreams - until they became mornings made of nightmarish POUR choices...

I'm talking to you, **Box Wine**. I bet you knew this song was about you. The sugar-filled headaches and vomit-filled toilets are no longer fun rites of passage into adulthood - they're reminders that "if it feels good, do it" is a shitty life strategy. I slapped the bag* again and again, and I was the only one who paid the price. I struggled to leave you behind, but I pulled on that old, stained hoodie one too many times as you glamoured me back into a blackout abyss.

I don't wear hoodies anymore. Especially not *that* one - it still reeks of regurgitated Cheetos.

I've changed. I've grown. I pour wine out of bottles and into glasses now, instead of opening a spigot and chugging to a chant. You're still living in your frat house glory days, playing video games in your mom's basement.

You belong to someone else now, and I don't judge her for loving you. I hope you bring her the pleasure that we both shared - without the pain of regret that only *I* suffered. You'll do what you always do: move on to intoxicate and toxify the next co-ed in a hoodie, and leave her body on the bathroom floor while her friends hold her hair back and say, "We *told* you not to see him again - when will you learn?"

My greatest years are ahead of me. Yours are... well, you'll always be where you were when we met - hanging out on a bottom shelf to be picked up by someone with no other options, or content with the consequences. I wish you all the best in your life - just not in my glass.

Refill & Reflect

POURsonality Trait:

Box Wine, you are my rock bottom. Much like with my actual toxic exes - my sweet tooth instantly sours and my stomach revolts at the thought of ever letting you in again.

If you enjoy box wine, you can stop here! Now, don't let me ruin your fling - it has its appeal and in some cases, it's actually trying hard to be less gross. But when it disappoints you, you can't say you weren't warned.

Are we still talking about the wine here...? That's up to you.

Sip Tip:

If you MUST drink box wine - I mean, there are absolutely no other options... at all. Here's what you do:

• Add ice, fruit and club soda- make it a spritzer!

• If you raid their liquor cabinet and find brandy, that spritzer is just a few glugs away from becoming sangria.

• Don't overdo it and alternate with water, and you might avoid the headache from all the added sugars and additives beyond the vineyard.

Share Your POUR Choice Story

Journal about your own toxic ex.

_____
_____
_____
_____
_____
_____
_____
_____
_____
_____
_____
_____
_____
_____
_____
_____
_____
_____
_____

Time To Wine About It!

Which wine pairs with your story: _____

Chapter 2

Feaux-Gettabout-It...

I hated your face the moment I saw you.

You were uptight, unapproachable, and reeked of elitist privilege. I knew all about you after talking to your other first dates, who never became a second. And let's be honest - you didn't like me either. You thought I was too loud, too crass, and had heard enough stories about me in my "bag-slapping" twenties to write me off without a second thought.

We glared at each other from across the room, daring the other to make the first move - if only to deliver the cutting one-liners we'd both locked and loaded in our heads, ready to fire if given the chance.

> ME: *"Maybe if you unclenched your ass cheeks, you'd make a real friend - not just bootlickers who think your family's greatness rubbed off on you."*
>
> HIM: *"If you stopped laughing like a hyena and cracking dirty dad jokes, I wouldn't be tempted to hand you a red Solo cup and direct you to the box wine table... on the lawn."*

Nope. We were *not* vibing. AT all.

You were old money, blue-blooded, legacy-branded entitlement in khaki pants - pants chosen by your grandmother, rightly so since she paid for them.. What a trust fund poser, resting on generational laurels while pretending to earn what your parents *actually* worked for.

You, in turn, saw me as chaos in a cocktail dress.

> **HIM:** *"She's eyeballing me like I'm the last Aperol Spritz in Italy. She doesn't think she's good enough for me - and she's right. I'll fake a polite smile if she approaches, but she's out of her league. Don't embarrass yourself, sweetheart."*
>
> **ME:** *"Why is he smirking at me like I'm supposed to swoon? He looks like a rich boy trying to cosplay* rugged. Casual smug isn't a vibe. You're not even interesting enough to hate, bro - and too simple to know or care. You're just boring."*

It was disdain at first sight that grew into disgust by the end of the night. We're still mentally insulting each other without uttering an actual sound.

> **HIM:** *"You can't afford me."*

ME: *"I would never overpay for you."*

HIM: *"Your palate isn't sophisticated enough to appreciate me."*

ME: *"You're a phony - and you are the only one who doesn't know it."*

Refill & Reflect

POURsonality Trait:

Hmph, he WISHES!

He doesn't have the structure to even develop a POURsonality.

I have this internal conversation every time I come across certain wines. Those brands remind me of those boys in high school who strutted around with cocksure confidence that only comes from being born into privilege and never made to develop on their own.

You know the ones. Fancy bottle. Big brand name with a big price tag to match, or marked down so far you think you've found a magic stash of mispriced treasure. If you see one of these bottles, beware!

Way too often, you'll find lower end versions of these expensive brand wines are actually made using more chemicals than grapes - and you can taste it. That's why they spend so much time & money marketing their legacy, so they can get people to buy into their image from decades past.

Call me spoiled, but I like my wine from a vineyard, not a science lab, although science IS precisely what makes wine into precious prized possession! But don't forget- science also creates monsters.

These are the wines that are often front and center at weddings and corporate events - impressing people either don't know better or don't drink wine often enough to care about the difference, and disappointing those who have experienced wine on the other side and taste through the facade.

They're the trust fund babies of the wine world - riding the coattails of their grandparents' greatness and phoning it in ever since.

 ## Sip Tip:

Don't take the bait!

Just because a wine has a well-known name and $100+ price tags in their portfolio doesn't mean *that* bottle you see is top tier. A lot of premium wineries produce lower-tier "entry wines" to reach a wider audience. That $40 version might be more like Kool-Aid than Cabernet.

So when you see a familiar luxury brand marked down at Costco and think, *"Wow, what a deal!"* - pause.

- Some big names sell their souls in bargain bins. It doesn't mean *all* their wine is trash - it just means some of it is riding on a reputation that it didn't earn.

- If it tastes the same, year after year, that's often achieved through chemical manipulation. These wines are often one dimensional - like a conversation with a shallow narcissist.

- When in doubt, seek out wines from boutique wineries or small lot wines from big name wineries.

Or just ask yourself: *Would this wine ever talk down to me at a party?* If the answer is yes, you already know - it's all veneer, no vintage.

Share Your POUR Choice Story

Journal about your own trust fund baby experience.

_____

_____

_____

_____

_____

_____

_____

_____

_____

_____

_____

_____

_____

_____

_____

_____

_____

_____

_____

_____

_____

_____

_____

Time To Wine About It!

Which wine pairs with your story: _____

Chapter 3

Fear Is a Factor

Fear is funny - not in a haha way, but in how it can either devour us, pecking away like turkey vultures on roadkill, or it can drive us to do hard things, like writing a book in less than 90 days.

A single moment in 1990 gave fear full control over my logical brain. A loud BANG at 5:36am jolted me awake gasping for air - I dreamed I had died in water. The fear stuck to me like stink on shit and became an irrational albatross around my neck.

I knew how to swim. Hell, I was already in the Navy and had passed the swim test. It made absolutely no sense! So, I confronted this new fear by white water rafting, tubing, cruises - you name it, but its barbed claws simply sank in deeper, dragging me to Davy Jones Locker* every time I was near anything bigger than a jacuzzi.

More nightmares. Constant tug of jumping overboard on cruises or pulling a Thelma and Louise, driving straight off of a bridge and into the ocean. The siren song is a real thing y'all and it was winning the battle for my life, stealing away moments and chipping away at my confidence.

I was sick of being controlled by it, making excuses to skip boat trips with friends, and panicking just looking at the deep end of a swimming pool.

For Don's 51st birthday, in January 2022, I got him the greatest gift EVER- swim lessons (for ME)! Yes, I'm the best wife ever.

I didn't know it when I booked her, but my swim coach ended up being a mindset coach as well.

I jumped in the pool covered in goggles, fins and sheer terror.

I froze, clinging to the wall for ten about minutes - my only movement was emptying tears from my goggles as the six-year-olds doggie paddled around me, for sure wondering why the weird old lady was crying in 4 feet of water.

With a giant sigh of resignation, I finally let go of the wall and let the floaty board thingy do its job to keep my head above water. Turns out, they really DO keep your head above water - huh!

Even though I survived - obviously - every class, I still had panic attacks each time I was back on land.

> **ME:** *"I'm just prolonging the inevitable, I should just let the water win."*
>
> **COACH:** *"Not on my watch."*

I refused to quit even though I cried before, during and after every class, heart racing like the rec center pool was filled with sharks and I was bloody bait.

But my coach kept turning the perspective around and around until something clicked.

> **COACH:** *"You are in control, Renee- 99% of you knows what to do and how to do it. That 1% is a liar & it doesn't even belong in your world. Visualize it, give it a face. Now PUNCH it dead in the mouth with your right hand, fill your lungs with life, push off of the wall and meet me at the other end of the pool. NOW."*

And I did. Over and over. And in June 2022, I WON.

Now, I jump into whatever body of water I am near just to lift a middle finger at Percy - that's what I call that 1% flea before I flick it away. I float, swim to the edge, then get back to my poolside wine. But there's more.

I subconsciously stopped freaking out from other fears that weighed me down. Flying bugs. Horses. Bees. Okay- spiders still send me into a high pitched panic, baby steps y'all.

Rejection. Judgement. Ridicule. They are someone else's problem now. Without hesitation, now I waltz into every room with a lighter step and confidence that a "no" just made room for the right YES. Instead of being afraid of not fitting in, I decide which rooms deserve me. It's not arrogance, it's recognition of what others see, that I finally believe.

I've officially relaxed into a life that is no longer ruled by fear.

Refill & Reflect

POURsonality Trait:

Hello darkness my old friend- you are the dreaded, intimidating Restaurant Wine List.

You used to make me feel like I was playing Russian Roulette with my meals and money. I was afraid to look foolish in front of my friends who said "YOU own a wine tour company - you pick the wine!"

I just knew that if I mispronounced Assyrtiko, the wait staff was pointing and laughing at our table behind my back. Just the thought of ordering a wine that tasted bitter with food because it wasn't a proper pairing brought bile to my throat. Which, fun fact, is ALSO bitter.

So with a deep breath, no goggles or fins, I wrestled you into submission. I OWN you, wine list.

> **ME (smiling at the water):** *"We're ordering the chicken parmesan and short rib risotto, which two wines would you choose from your wine list?"*
>
> **WAITER:** *"Uhhh, let me get the Sommelier, I'm not sure."*

Look who's laughing now... NO ONE. You don't need a wine certification to beat the list- you just need the ovarian audacity and testicular fortitude to ask questions.

🍷 Sip Tip:

Most people know as much about wine as you do unless they study it with a manic obsession. Fun fact: even we oenophiles still only know a fraction of what there is to learn.

It's not a rich, old, white, boys club anymore, so if you don't fit that bill- don't worry, and if you DO fit that bill, scoot over- your world just got a whole lot more interesting! You're welcome- and- welcome to stay.

We all get to enjoy the beauty that comes with a well-chosen wine and food pairing. And we are all welcome to learn one meal at a time with these simple tips:

- Look at the wine priced in the middle. Sometimes they are just as well made as the more expensive wines and the margins are great for the restaurant.

- Don't be afraid to request a taste before purchasing a bottle. Any wine available by the glass should be an option to try first. Don't like it? Don't buy it. The waiter didn't make the damn wine - he won't be offended.

- If they open a bottle and you don't like it, speak up. A good Somm will taste it, determine if it's off, needs aeration, or just isn't to your liking.

    Remember that sometimes it just needs time to breathe- exposure to oxygen will change the balance of what you taste, especially in older vintages.

Or, the right food brings out its best features-Sangiovese and Arneis for example, love acidic foods to tamp down their own high acidity.

- What grows together goes together. Choose a wine from the region of your cuisine, or one with a similar climate to hedge your bets on picking a winner.

Share Your POUR Choice Story

Journal about your own fear-conquering experience.

_____

_____

_____

_____

_____

_____

_____

_____

_____

_____

_____

_____

_____

_____

_____

_____

_____

_____

_____

_____

_____

Time To Wine About It!

Which wine pairs with your story: _____

Chapter 4

Blinded By The Light

Actually, I *wish* I had been blinded, but sadly, it was just the opposite. The light revealed what the darkness concealed, and the regret and shame were tough to bear.

It was 1990, I was stationed just south of Munich in Germany and living what I thought was my best life. At the time- it WAS. This energetic cheerleader from Bellevue, Nebraska was now a Navy Petty Officer on a tiny base with an important mission- I was on top of the world!

Nightclubbing alone was my THING. I hated going out with people who didn't think dancing until the lights came up at 4am was a wise move when you had to report for duty at 6am. You leave the dance floor covered in sweat, wolf down some bad gas station food since nothing else is open, change into your uniform at stoplights, then stroll into work, wiping the club stamp off your wrist as you sign in. Where's the problem?

But alas, this led to some monumental POUR choices.

He looked so cool, chilling at the bar in a white blazer and black pants, with that "I'm a rich European man" casual style. Black slicked back hair, strong jawline, and piercing blue eyes that were staring my way.

I put on a dance floor show targeted at him, shaking my tail feathers to the pounding techno bass. I glance over at my conquest-to-be, and sure enough, he held up a drink and beckoned me over with a tilt of his head. I turned up my kittenish smile and sashayed his way.

POUR CHOICE #1: Taking a drink from a stranger at a crowded nightclub.

It was tequila and grapefruit, my favorite back then. The club was loud and dark, except for those sweeping lights, so we had to speak closely into each other's ears.

ME: *"Thank you for the drink- where are you from?"*

HIM: *"Sorry I speak no much english."*

ME (in German): *"Do you speak German?"*

HIIM (in English): *"Leetle beet. English more."*

Internally I sighed, this wasn't going to be easy, but he was hot enough to make the effort. Through nightclub sign language I figured out he was Greek. His brooding eyes unapologetically and appreciatively swept up and down my body constantly- I don't think he knew I had a face. But I didn't care- I was 20, in great shape, and looking for Mr. Right Now.

No more talking. We danced, flirted and eventually made out. Ugh- he's a smoker... eh, I can deal with it. He yelled into my ear- "We go now?"

POUR CHOICE #2: I go. I followed the stranger out of the club to his flat nearby.

He didn't turn on the lights- the moon was enough. It smelled like expensive cologne and sandalwood, and I was excited about my first European fling- maybe he actually owns a yacht and this is a crash pad, one of hundreds he had around the world... sooo mysterious...let's party.

Needless to say there wasn't much talking once we got there- and sadly, there wasn't much of anything else either. Turns out foreplay was ONEplay, and he wasn't up to the task he was assigned, and was snoring as I stared at the ceiling and thought, "THAT'S IT?"

Bad breath, worse bedroom skills and no food. I made a BIG mistake and needed to get gone- a gas station hot dog was waiting for me somewhere out there and I had to be at work in two hours. I slid out of the bed and searched for my clothes as quietly as I could. He stirred.

HIM: *"You go now?"*

ME: *"I go now. Work! You have light?"*

<u>**POUR CHOICE #3:**</u> The light.

He reaches for a lighter on the nightsand.

ME: *"No, LIGHT."* I pointed to the sky in more nightclub sign language.

HIM: *"Ahh, yes!"*

The lamp flickered on and I had to physically stop myself from jumping back. That slicked back hair hid a balding cul de sac on top of his head. The broad shoulders came from shoulder pads- he was skinny, pale and honestly? Looked like he needed an IV full of vitamins, STAT. But the worst was yet to come…

He lit a cigarette, inhaled deeply then reclined on the pillow as he blew smoke my way. His face was covered in greasy acne scars, what I thought were mysterious eyes in the club were actually a unibrow and a lazy wandering left eye- how did I miss THAT?

Then he smiled, and it looked like his tongue was in jail. Crooked, missing teeth, and now I know what the strange sensation was when we kissed- dry chapped lips that a vat of Burts Bees likely couldn't save.

I busied myself getting dressed while holding back the vomit rising from my gut.

HIM: *"We meet more?"*

ME (over my shoulder as I make a beeline for the door): *"Uh, yeah. I call you!"*

I boogied to my car, ate all the breath mints I could find, skipped the gas station and went straight back to the barracks to scrub every ounce of him from my body. The first SMART decision I had made in the last 4 hours.

Refill & Reflect

POURsonality Trait:

Two Buck Chuck, hey buddy! Your label was so cute, I had to bring you home with me. I thought it would be a fun adventure to get to know you. I was wrong, behind the label was a sour, ugly indefinable "wine" that reeked of rotten grapes and disappointment. I did the walk of shame, hiding you in the bottom of the trash so no one could see my mistake.

Sip Tip:

Sometimes when you shoot your shot, it's an airball with no chance at scoring. If you are two buck chuck (TBC) shopping- hedge the bets in your favor:

- Keep your expectations low- TBC won't change your life, but it can fill the need. And if it sucks, at least you aren't out much cash.
- Hate it? Cook with it. Unless it's actually faulty and tastes like the bottom of a Grecian ashtray, throw a small amount into a sauce, and the rest into the trash. You deserve better.

- Look beyond the label- is the varietal one the region is known for, or is it an obscure grape or unspecified blend? At this price point you are better off choosing a region that matches the varietal: California Cab, Italian Sangiovese (usually Chianti), Argentinian Malbec, Australian Shiraz.

Basically- turn on the light before you take it home.

Share Your POUR Choice Story

Journal about a time the lights come on to reveal a POUR choice you wish you could unsee - or un-choose.

_____

_____
_____
_____
_____
_____
_____
_____
_____
_____
_____
_____
_____
_____
_____
_____
_____
_____
_____
_____
_____

Time To Wine About It!

Which wine pairs with your story: _____

Part II: Wine Fridge

Every POUR Choice has a shelf life. Some are right for now, others are right forever. These relationships may have a shorter shelf life IN your life, but they bring smiles to your heart as memories, even after their time has passed.

Take a sip down memory lane with me, through relationship choices that I am glad I made, even if they faded with time.

Their impact shapes our lives as much as the DUMP BUCKET, but without the regret.

Chapter 5

Business Blends Beyond Friends

They tell you when your slip is showing. They don't let you go on stage wearing something that makes you look frumpy or dumpy. And they DEFINITELY don't serve you broccoli and tell you it's greens*.

They are your Biz Besties (BBs), and they change the game - how? By forming strong Bizlationships®. **Bizlationships* are business connections that are mutually beneficial and drive revenue generating collaborations.**

I spent decades without BBs in my life - not just because my trust issues and control freak tendencies drive my desire to be a solo act, but also because, well… I AM A LOT. Ideas flow through my mind faster than I can keep up with, so I talk really fast and tend to combine thoughts that don't belong together. Imagine a chef who makes dessert while finishing the main course and accidentally puts sugar in the gravy instead of salt… true story. Don't let me cook for you.

My impatience makes me do it myself rather than teach someone else how. Where most people see walls that put their business in a box, I see windows with opportunities on the other side. I usually dive through them headfirst, making those around me feel scared for their safety and unsure about my mental state.

Even though I'm usually an extroverted extrovert, I've always been a loner in business- I felt like others simply didn't get me. But as I grew my businesses, that "go it alone" strategy became unsustainable. I was no longer a proud solopreneur- I was just lonely and stuck. I told myself I was "methodically planning my next steps," but the truth? I was as stagnant as a Mississippi swamp on a windless, sweltering summer day.

I had no one to tell me what I didn't know that I didn't know. Dr. Google and wild-ass guesses had taken me as far as they could.

But then, something wild happened. At 52 years old, I discovered a tribe of people who were - somehow - just like me. And honestly, that was terrifying. They thought faster than most. They weren't afraid to take calculated risks. Some of them even cursed like sailors, matching my f-bombs and filter-free responses. They didn't just keep up with my vision - they elevated it with next-level ideas and resources I didn't even know I needed.

They were also the opposite of me in all the right ways. Where I lagged, they flourished. Where they struggled, I soared. I brought creativity to the table that was set with their logic.

What a relief and a rush to be in that room! I had grown so used to doing things the hard way, it was second nature to kamikaze my way into the unknown by diving through windows. But my Biz Besties opened doors I didn't even know existed - and together, we reached shared goals without being covered in shattered glass.

(Now, you may be asking yourself, "Why didn't Renee just open the damn window?" Did you read the part about my impatience?? That's why. I'd rather pick glass out of my hair than jiggle a rusty window latch.)

My BBs and I don't **gatekeep*** - in fact, we shout each other's greatness from the rooftops and share opportunities. We're on the same team. When one of us wins, we all win. When one of us drops the ball, we *all* feel it. So we work together to bring out the best in each other.

We don't compete for the spotlight - we light each other up so we all shine brighter. Even if two of us share the same strengths, egos don't get in the way. Strengths ebb and flow, and we all leave the room better than we found it.

Sure, we could each stand alone in our expertise and be a force to be reckoned with. But together?

We are LEGENDARY.

Refill & Reflect

POURsonality Trait:

Oh Bordeaux, this blend is for YOU!

Your reds are represented by Petit Verdot, Malbec, Merlot, Cabernet Franc, and Cabernet Sauvignon - some of the world's most recognizable and respected varietals.

Each one can stand alone, but together? Iconic.

The blend varies depending on your flavor goals. More plum? Less cedar? Filet with fingerling potatoes? Roasted pork and green bean casserole? (Please God, not green bean casserole - does anyone *actually* eat that?)

Same with your BBs- focus on finance, with a dash of marketing? Heavier on sales with a side of content creation- or vice versa?

Bordeaux blends turn any occasion into a special occasion, from your $500 a head fundraising gala, to your intimate dinner with your BBs at the table. Pop that bottle for your supportive sisters and backbone brothers - because without them, you're just another lonely bottle collecting dust on a shelf.

Sip Tip:
How to Choose a Bordeaux Blend

Just like some of your Biz Besties are better suited for certain audiences, Bordeaux wines are the same. Both present and age beautifully, but appeal to different tastes- just like your Besties:

- If you love fruitier or younger wines, start with Right Bank. The wines are less tannic, silkier and softer in general than Left Bank wines, and are Merlot driven.

- Like your reds big, bold, and capable of punching you in the mouth…? Left Bank Bordeaux blends lead with Cabernet Sauvignon, and are powerful palate pleasers.

Share Your POUR Choice Story

Journal about your own biz besties.

_____

_____

_____

_____

_____

_____

_____

_____

_____

_____

_____

_____

_____

_____

_____

_____

_____

_____

_____

_____

Time To Wine About It!

Which wine pairs with your story: _____

Chapter 6
Lost In Translation

There was that time I tried to remember how to say "cheers" in Estonian. You'd think it wouldn't be that hard - Google Translate exists, there are language apps galore, and our neighbor is *literally* from Estonia. But no. I managed to make a toast that insulted someone's ancestors.

Let me set the scene.

Don, my husband of over 30 years (you'll meet him later), and I were heading across the driveway to have dinner with our new neighbors, Marci and Steve. We brought a Virginia Viognier to pair with baked cheesy appetizers and a Chianti Classico for the smoked pork with tomato gravy. It was going to be a culinary coup: wine, food, and guiding our new friends through our little slice of suburban heaven.

By bottle four, the wine was flowing and so was the conversation. And, as I always do when meeting someone from another country, I got curious. Marci shared stories of her homeland and I was enthralled, missing my years stationed in Germany.

ME: *"Wait - before we drink, how do you say 'cheers' in Estonian?"*

MARCI: *"It's kind of tricky, but it sounds like a dirty word. That'll help you remember!"*

Dirty word? She was speaking my language... Marci raised her glass, said it, we all repeated it, wine down the hatch and then butts to their deck to enjoy the summer breezes. Steve played "Hotel California" on guitar while Marci and I drunkenly rewrote the lyrics in what I still believe is the superior version:

"Mirrors on the ceiling, Closets full of mice -

We are all just prisoners here -   You should roll the dice..."

Glorious.

A few months later, they invited us to a dinner party with extended family and friends. I was READY. I rehearsed my Estonian "cheers" line over and over while selecting the perfect wines: a crisp Sicilian Grillo and a bold Oregon Pinot Noir.

As we headed across the driveway, I felt a gentle hand on my arm.

DON (kindly): *""NeNe, please don't try to say cheers in Estonian again. You don't remember it right,* *and I think you might be calling someone's grandmother a goat."*

ME (confidently): *"Puh-lease. I GOT this."*

But I didn't GOT that.

At dinner, everything went beautifully. Laughter. Warm vibes. Plates passed, wine poured. I stood up, glass in hand, and declared: *"I'd like to thank our hosts for a beautiful evening - by saying cheers in Estonian!"*

Marci smiled, expecting the best. Don looked down, expecting the worst. And I, with full conviction, raised my glass and declared: *"Sook-a-DEEK!"*

Silence.

Marci, sweetly confused: *"I'm sorry… what did you say?"*

I cleared my throat and tried again, shifting the emphasis:

"SOOK-a-deek!"

Marci blinked in schock. *"No, no, Renee. It's Terviseks. Sounds like 'dirty sex!' Not whatever that was."*

Without missing a beat, Steve chimed in: "I like Renee's version better. Sook-a-DEEK, y'all!"

We all *died* laughing. Even Steve's mom, bless her soul, was in stitches. I had unintentionally propositioned everyone at the table to have an orgy - and it became an instant classic.

To this day, we're still close friends and neighbors. Even after I accidentally told Steve's mom to "sook-a-deek" the first time I met her... and it's how we toast evenings on the deck with raised glasses and bad karaoke.

Refill & Reflect

POURsonality Trait:

Chardonnay is a deeply misunderstood grape that often presents a loved or hated flavor in wine: butter.

Many people assume the buttery taste in Chardonnay comes from oak, but that couldn't be further from true. Wine geekery alert!

Oak adds body, baking spices, and richness.

Butter comes from a process called **Malolactic Fermentation** (MLF or "malo"), where tart malic acid (think green apples) is converted into creamy lactic acid (think yogurt or milk). Nearly all red wines go through MLF, but tannins and other flavors replace butter, and the creaminess is usually more noticeable in white wines - notably Chardonnay.

The result? Silky texture. Buttery notes. A smooth, almost oily mouthfeel. But stop blaming- or crediting- oak, you're barking up the wrong tree.

Sip Tip:

That butter you love? It's science, baby, and it pairs beautifully with popcorn! But don't expect it in every Chardonnay.

- The only region where every Chardonnay goes through MLF in Burgundy
- Even unoaked stainless steel Chards can go through or skip MLF
- Look for words like crisp and bright to describe Chards with no MLF
- Silky and creamy are descriptors that indicate malo in many wines- not just Chardonnay.

Share Your POUR Choice Story

Journal about your sook-a-deek moment.

_____
_____
_____
_____
_____
_____
_____
_____
_____
_____
_____
_____
_____
_____
_____
_____
_____
_____
_____
_____

Time To Wine About It!

Which wine pairs with your story: _____

Chapter 7
Booty Call

There are times when you just want to be the little spoon at night - but not the next morning. You're not looking for fireworks and forever. You just want an exhilarating release that only lasts a few hours. A break from the chaos. A fling, not a foundation.

You want a **Booty Call**.

That one-night stand you can stand for more than one night - but only *one night at a time.*

When I take you to parties, you sparkle just enough to make everyone feel comfortable in your presence. You're charming but not clingy, there's no trauma dump. Just a lighthearted hang with someone who knows exactly why they're there - and exactly when to bounce.

Thank you for not wanting to move in with me or sit me down for DTR* talks. There's no pressure to make you breakfast.

You just show up, we do our thing that we do SO well, and you leave before sunrise without leaving a dent in my pillow..

Oh, how I adore that, even after the 50th call, you're just as delightful as you were on the first ring.

Heyyyy Pinot Grigio, how YOU doin'? Come slide into my DMs!

I reach for you at WineauxClock when I don't want to commit to pairing with a meal or spend each sip analyzing secondary flavors and tertiary finishes. You're a laid-back crowd pleaser, like a song by Sugar Ray or Marvin Gaye.

I can pour Pinot Grigio (PiGri) into a red Solo cup without guilt, and pair it with apps, not four course meals. As PiGri slips on their shoes and slips out the door before the sun peeks over the horizon, you laugh at a joke only the two of you understand.

There's no awkwardly hopeful "Call me tomorrow…?" No longing glances. Just good times, good vibes, and maybe a quick thanks-for-the-good-time, check-ya-later text. Short, sweet and satisfying - just like this chapter.

R<small>EFILL</small> & R<small>EFLECT</small>

POUR<small>SONALITY</small> T<small>RAIT</small>:

Pinot Grigio, you are my favorite Booty Call. My Mr. Right Now. You're always easy to access. You're predictable, in the best possible way. You always know how to please me. You don't overcomplicate things - you keep it light, bright, then call it a night.

Sip Tip:

Pinot Grigio is a classic porch pounder*. You can find great bottles for under $20 - and even under $10 if you know where to look. But be warned: not all inexpensive Pinot Grigios are created equal.

To avoid chemical-tasting PiGri imposters, look for:

- **delle Venezie DOC** (Northeast Italy): clean, crisp, and affordable

- **Grauburgunder** (Germany): nuanced minerality with a bit more texture

- **Pinot Gris** (Alsace): richer, rounder, and full-bodied

Same grape. Different vibes. Choose your adventure.

Share Your POUR Choice Story

Journal about your own booty call experience.

_____
_____
_____
_____
_____
_____
_____
_____
_____
_____
_____
_____
_____
_____
_____
_____
_____
_____
_____
_____
_____
_____

Time To Wine About It!

Which wine pairs with your story: _____

PART III: WINE CELLAR

Then there are POUR choices that never cease to flow through your life, veins and heart. The kind of connections that stand the test of time and breathe as long as you do.

They are rare, unique and unrivaled for the space in your world that belongs only to them, never to be removed or replaced. Only a select few bottles are cellar-worthy, just like only a select few humans can be called your inner circle.

Cheers to exploring the wine cellar of our lives as we pop the cork on their influence in our worlds, and savor every age-worthy, complex sip they bring us.

Chapter 8
Love at First Sip

Ready to hear my epic love at first sip story?

ME *(telling the story)*: *"I loved him before I even saw his face. Not in the fairytale way. Not in the "I saw him across the room and the heavens parted" kind of way.*

More like - something in the air shifted. A tingle. A charge. A gut feeling that said: this one's different.

I thought I knew what love was. I'd convinced myself I'd been in love at least four times before. But this feeling?

This became unicorn-level magic. The toe-tingling, hair-on-your-arms standing up, light-you-up-from-the-inside kind of love. And it scared the shit out of me."

HIM *(telling the story)*: *"She came busting through the doors late - books in one hand, coffee in the other, and loud apologies flying in every direction. The Chief barked, "Nobody cares - you're late. Take a seat."*

And she did. With zero shame, maximum charm, and a smile that reached her eyes..

She was chaos in a uniform. A literal hot mess. And I could not look away."

We were both 22 year old sailors who just arrived at our second duty station in the US Navy, ready to party our way through Rota, Spain. We were single and ready for belt notching, Spanish speaking, late night adventures.

Definitely not looking for forever. But when our eyes met, it was game on.

Our flirtation was childish, ridiculous, and honestly - kind of adorable.

> **HIM *(making chomping noises as I walked by)*:** "Damn girl, those dungarees are working overtime. Hungry butt alert."
>
> **ME *(rolling my eyes)*:** "Oh please. Try a new line, everyone's dungarees crawl up their ass when they walk. And don't call me girl! Say my name, or say nothing at all."
>
> **HIM:** "Daaammn, I'm just saying... if you're gonna sashay, don't blame me for staring."
>
> **ME:** "Keep dreaming. I'd make you forget your own name."

(Cue dramatic dungaree wedgie removal and exit stage left. 😉)

We flirted for weeks.

Then came the turning point: a nasty lunch that led to the first of endless dinners.

I lived on ramen noodles with random proteins (think canned chicken or hot dogs). I was broke, creative, and usually proud of my innovative concoctions that cost less than a dollar to make.

> **HIM *(nose wrinkled in disgust)*:** *"Is that tuna ramen again? Girl, I mean RENEE, that's criminal."*
>
> **ME:** *"It's survival. Got something better to offer?"*
>
> **HIM:** *"You know I do. What's your specialty? Green bean casserole with a sprinkle of sadness?"*
>
> **ME (challenged):** *"Tuesday. My place. You'll shut up after one bite."*
>
> **HIM:** *"I'll be there, but I'll eat first - just in case."*
>
> **ME (eyes rolling):** *"Keep it up and my butt won't be the only thing hungry!"*

Game on! Oh SHIT- GAME. ON.

I biked three miles from the base to my beach apartment that day with turkey cutlets, broccoli, potatoes, and the equivalent $0.75 left to my name. I still needed wine.

So I bought the cheapest- and only- wine in the bodega: a box called **El Molino** - which, conveniently, was also the name of my apartment building. It felt like a sign.

He showed up with flowers. Smelled dinner. Smirked appreciatively, my god is that a dimple? He's SO cute out of uniform... breathe Renee... play it cool.

> **HIM**: *"Smells amazing. What can I do to help?"*
>
> **ME**: *"Thank you! I was out of ramen. You can open the wine."*
>
> **HIM**: *"You got a corkscrew?"*
>
> **ME**: *"Wow you're bougie! Don't need one...HERE."*

I handed him the box, scissors, and two mismatched water glasses.

He snipped off the corner, sniffed the cardboard triangle, and locked eyes with me.

> **HIM** *(mock-sophisticated, pinkie up)*: *"Ah yes, a very good week for this one."*

That's when it happened.

The shared laugh. The chemistry spark. The stomach fluttering look. We never recovered - and we never wanted to.

We kissed for the first time on April Fool's Day, 1993.

This booty call was an epic fail. We've been dating ever since, and didn't stop even after we married in November 1994.

Refill & Reflect

POURsonality Trait:

We are Old Vine Zin. Bold. Spicy. A little wild in our youth. But deep-rooted. Rare. Better with time.

We're not for everyone. But for each other? *Perfectly paired.*

We've evolved from shot-taking party kids to house-party hosts with curated playlists, artisan snacks and a 300+ bottle wine collection. We still tease. We still flirt. And we *definitely* still laugh.

Old Vine Zin doesn't rush. It ripens slowly. It holds history in every drop. It pairs best with layered flavors, unapologetic conversations, and people who can handle the intensity. And a few well placed wisecracks since ballbusting is our love language.

Sip Tip:

If you want to fall in love with Old Vine Zin, head to Sonoma. Wellington Cellars has vines dating back to 1882 - and the fruit they bear? Worthy of anniversaries, fireside chats, and falling in love all over again.

Share Your POUR Choice Story

Journal about your love at first sip.

_____

_____

_____

_____

_____

_____

_____

_____

_____

_____

_____

_____

_____

_____

_____

_____

_____

_____

_____

_____

_____

Time To Wine About It!

Which wine pairs with your story: _____

Chapter 9
Ride Or Die

You never judge me.

You just show up with bail money, clean underwear, and absolutely no questions.

You get me in a way no one else does. You're the first one to pile on unsolicited praise, reminding me of my value even as I'm pulling a lint-covered Jolly Rancher from the bottom of my purse, contemplating the risk vs reward of popping it into my mouth.

At parties, you *always* shine the light in my direction:

> YOU: *"I'm hosting a cocktail party and have no clue what to serve with the champagne. Renee, any ideas?"*
>
> ME: *"Ohhh, YES. A best-kept secret: fried chicken. Trust me. The salt and fat in the chicken are a natural fit for Champagne or Cava.*
>
> *If you're serving Prosecco or sparkling Viognier - try popcorn popped in bacon grease. Instant hero status - just check your guest list for vegetarians and Muslims first!"*

YOU: *"That's brilliant!"*

ME (blushing, slightly): *"Thank you, friend - brilliance recognizes brilliance."*

But I don't love you just because you boost my ego. You are so well loved because you are the real deal. You make everyone around you feel like they matter. You never fake a compliment. You don't play games. You're that rare mix of popular *and* grounded.

Even with all your star power, you're happy to be the backup singer if it makes the whole performance better. You don't try to hog the spotlight - but you damn well *deserve* it.

You are my **Ride or Die**.

You show up in sneakers and a hoodie one day, and a ballgown the next. You're that friend who's equally comfortable singing karaoke in a dive bar or walking a red carpet - and you make *both* look good.

Our friendship is old school, beyond pokes, likes, and emojis. It thrives on inside jokes, hugs and lunches that last til dinner. It doesn't need to talk every day- it knows we're never far from each other's thoughts. And it never, ever asks the other to compromise their principles- shared morals are part of our love for each other.

Sometimes this bond is by blood, sometimes it's by choice. It could be next door, or miles and continents may separate you from me. But one thing's for sure: I'm YOUR Ride or Die too. Deejay, cue up "That's What Friends Are For"... and hand each of us a mic.

Refill & Reflect

POURsonality Trait:

Salute to Cabernet Sauvignon, for your old world charm and new world glamour, for your humble confidence despite your obvious talent. You're poured for presidents then sipped at backyard BBQs.

You're iconic yet approachable, and never feel out of place. You don't need backup - but you harmonize with the best of them. You're the heart that beats in Bordeaux blends, Super Tuscans, and California reds. That's Ride or Die, Big Sip Energy.

Sip Tip:

Many wine regions allow a bottle to be labeled as a single varietal if that grape makes up at least 75-85% of the wine. That means your "Merlot" or "Malbec" may still have a solid dose of Cab Sauv inside, adding structure, body, and longevity.

If you ever find yourself stranded on a desert island and can only choose one grape to sip forever?

Choose Cab Sauv. It's always got your back.

Share Your POUR Choice Story

Journal about your own ride or die.

_____
_____
_____
_____
_____
_____
_____
_____
_____
_____
_____
_____
_____
_____
_____
_____
_____
_____
_____
_____
_____
_____
_____

Time To Wine About It!

Which wine pairs with your story: _____

CHAPTER 10
WHY YOU SO SALTY?

We've all met those people who at first sight we think- "Damn, they look PISSED." I'm not just talking about Goliath syndrome, the male equivalent to resting bitch face- I'm talking about people who genuinely seem like the weight of the world is on their shoulders and you either want to run up and give them a big hug or give them wide berth and stay far, far away from what might be a donkey on the edge.

I chose to go in for the hug. Twice. Once in Spain, and once in Virginia.

BIG GRUMPY

Picture it: 1993, I had just arrived at the naval base in Rota Spain at the ripe young age of 22. It's where I first met Don Ventrice, who is now my "booty call fail" of a husband for thirty years and counting, but at this moment in time, he was just an irritating flirtation. You know how grains of sand itch their way into becoming a priceless pearl? We were juuuust starting to scratch that itch. but that's a separate POUR Relationship Choice, I digress.

While a group of us were waiting for our job assignments, in walks a guy who was as grumpy as he was tall- he was impossible to ignore. He towered over everyone else and his gloomy presence filled the room.

> **DON (whispering to me):** *"Damn-who's that grumpy ass dude over there?"*

> **ME (leaning in closer than necessary so he could smell my perfume):** *"Dunno- never seen him before, but it looks like someone pissed in his corn flakes."*

> **DON (chuckling and leaning in closer):** *"Word. What's that scent you're wearing- did you dab ramen noodle juice behind your ears?"*

Big Grumpy kept to himself and communicated mainly in annoyed exhalations and grouchy grunts if he bothered to acknowledge you at all. Don and I ran into him now and then through mutual buddies while partying out in town. He and Don slowly became friends while my romance with Don was in full bloom.

> **HIM:** *"We're headed to Torremolinos to party this weekend- you coming?"*

> **DON**: *"Yeah Renee and I are coming - gonna be a blast!"*
>
> **HIM**: *"Dude, why are you bringing sand to the BEACH? There will be gorgeous women everywhere!"*
>
> **DON**: *"Don't sweat it man, she's cool. For me it's BYOB- Bring Your Own Beach!"*

Needless to say- he and I did NOT become friends as fast as he and Don did. Sand at the BEACH? I'll show HIM a beach...

I went in for the "hug", and charmed him into accepting me as one of the guys when we all hung out, and as my security detail when Don had to work night shifts.

BIG ANGRY

The second time was in Virginia, picture it- 2012 on the baseball fields of Loudoun County. Our son played baseball for Briar Woods High School and on a high level travel team, and there were all types of personalities for us to observe, discuss and judge, our favorite pastime through the decades.

Dads frothing at the mouth when there was a bad call. The moms sharing chardonnay disguised in water bottles as "energy drinks". The parents pacing the fence on their cell phones, working between pitches. And then, there was THIS guy.

> **ME:** *"Yooo- check out that big angry dude at the fence!"*
>
> **DON:** *"How could I miss him? There are villagers with pitchforks waiting for him in the outfield!"*
>
> **ME:** *"I think his pet might be Babe the Big Blue Ox!"*
>
> **DON:** *"I don't get it…"*
>
> **ME:** *"You know, Paul Bunyan… the lumberjack! Didn't you read as a kid?"*
>
> **DON:** *"Nah, I was busy learning to cook food other than ramen noodles."*

Big Angry was a serious guy. Arms crossed. Face uncracked by smile lines. A real barrel of laughs. And his son was a really good ball player, so he took every pitch, play and moment seriously.

Eventually the team started traveling together, and we got to know him, whether he liked it or not. Team dinners, tailgates between double headers- nothing stops me when I decide to go in for the hug.

> **ME (smiling up at him at dinner):** *"Sooo, where are you from?"*

HIM (still polishing off wings without looking down at me): *"Kansas."*

ME: *"Whaaat- I grew up in Nebraska! We're practically neighbors!"*

HIM: *"HMPH."* **He looked down at my fries.** *"You gonna finish those?"*

ME (grinning like an idiot): *"Nope, have at em!"*

More baseball. More dinners. More shared fries. He began to thaw. (Like I gave him a choice.) Don broke through first, as usual, and the friendship with Big Angry evolved.

We didn't know then that both of these men would become two of our dearest friends, people we could count on and would travel with. Men who, beneath the tough, flinty exteriors were kind, generous and often hilarious people. And that side of them was revealed by their better halves. *(Who knows where this is going?)*

A foot and a half below their chins was where you found that soft yet powerful influence of their beautiful wives, who balanced them out perfectly, smoothed their rough edges, and made them palatable to the rest of the world. They turned Big Grumpy and Big Angry into gigantic teddy bears with their light hearted approach to life, fun personalities, and the wisdom that only a partner who has shared your life for decades can bring. Oh and they also whip the big guys' asses into shape with just one look. They ARE my people.

REFILL & REFLECT

POURsonality Trait:

Meet Albariño- it's that happy couple you love to hang out with. The dynamic between them is a perfect blend of acidity and citrus spritz, salinity and sweetness, and unexpected nuances that show up in the moment.

When you meet Albariño at first sip, you might be overwhelmed by the salty, mineral notes, but by the time you reach its finish - mellow fruit characteristics add balance and flavor, like pineapple on pork, or watermelon touched with sea salt.

Give Albariño a chance. You might not understand it at first, but with the right circumstances, you'll make a friend for life that pairs with the beaches of Spain, french fries in Virginia, and warm, unavoidable hugs.

Sip Tip:

Serve Albariño pretty cold. Let that first sip linger under your tongue for about 5 seconds, and let it touch both cheeks before swallowing. That next sip will be fruitier and a fuller expression of this glorious grape's character!

Share Your POUR Choice Story

Journal about someone who surprised you.

_____
_____
_____
_____
_____
_____
_____
_____
_____
_____
_____
_____
_____
_____
_____
_____
_____
_____
_____
_____

Time To Wine About It!

Which wine pairs with your story: _____

Chapter II

S-motherly Love

It's the warm, endless hug after a heartbreak.

It's the kind of love that smells like Sunday pot roast and sounds like soap operas blaring in the background while she has you on speakerphone.

It's not always graceful, and definitely not always subtle - but it's real. It's deep. It's permanent.

It's S-motherly Love.

The kind of love that comforts and protects. That nags, meddles, and inserts itself into conversations where it maybe (okay, definitely) wasn't invited. Not because it wants to control you - but because it *remembers what it was like to be you.*

It wants to shield you from every bruise, mistake, and regret. And sure, sometimes it suffocates you in the process. But it comes from the softest center of the heart.

When it's overbearing, s-mothering you with unsolicited advice? It's just trying to save you from the same mistakes it made.

When it's intrusive, jumping in to solve problems you didn't ask it to fix? It just wants you to be happy.

When it seems aloof, hanging back when you *really* wish it would swoop in and fix everything? It's just trying not to be called s-mothering and intrusive again.

This love seems complicated - but it's actually quite simple, and it never leaves your side. Even when it's quiet, it's still there.

This love turns meals into memories.

It sneaks healthy ingredients into your favorite dishes and seasons every meal with the stories you'll tell your own kids one day.

It's chili with cornbread and melted honey butter on snow days, thawing your cheeks after snowball fights.

It's the kind of love that never needs to say, "Remember me?" - because it's woven into who you are.

Sometimes, your S-mother plays the silent supporting actress role. She's the meal that gave you energy to hit a home run. She's the back rub that soothed you to sleep the night before a big test.

And when it's your moment - she's leading the chants, holding up the signs, and cheering the loudest from the stands.

When athletes win a championship, who do they thank first? That's right - **MOM**.

Because we hold it down so they can rise up.

Refill & Reflect

POURsonality Trait:

Thank you, **Merlot**, for being the Somm of moms.

The one who gets overlooked and under appreciated (looking at you, *Sideways*.) and yet…

You're always there, smoothing the rough edges, softening the sting, rounding out the blend.

Cabernet might steal the headlines, but it's your steady presence that makes the magic happen.

You're the warmth behind the boldness. The nurture behind the structure.

You're the one we turn to when we're tired, heart-worn, and in need of something familiar.

You don't need constant praise - our success is your win.

Sip Tip:

If you've sworn off Merlot, don't listen to Miles- (yeah Sideways, still talking to you) give it another chance. And chances are it's in many Cab Sauvs you drink without being listed on the label.

- Right-bank Bordeaux if you want to go straight to the top

- Washington State Merlot from the Walla Walla AVA

- Ease in with a Cab Sauv / Merlot blend from California or a Super Tuscan from Italy

OH! and PS: Call your mom and tell her you love her. No, not a text... <u>call</u> her! *(She's gonna call as soon as she sees a text from you anyway.)*

Share Your POUR Choice Story

Journal about your own s-motherly love.

_____

_____
_____
_____
_____
_____
_____
_____
_____
_____
_____
_____
_____
_____
_____
_____
_____
_____
_____
_____
_____
_____
_____
_____

Time To Wine About It!

Which wine pairs with your story: _____

Chapter 12
Puzzles & The Patriarch

I had two hernia surgeries by the time I was 15. Normally, that wouldn't be worth mentioning - except those surgeries were a turning point in an unexpected manner. They uncorked a bond with my father that's only grown stronger over the decades.

I can't remember a time when I wasn't a daddy's girl. He always knew me. He called me "little mouse girl" because I loved cheese. Back then it was Kraft singles. Now it's aged Gouda. But to a mouse? Cheese is cheese.

He helped me with homework, not by doing it for me, but by making it make sense when I struggled to understand it. Where other people saw a kid who couldn't think in a straight line, my Daddyo saw someone worth walking into the woods with - trusting we'd find our way out together.

He never said "just trust me and turn left." Instead, he rewrote the map so I could still arrive at the right answer, even if I took the scenic, loopy, totally illogical route. He made *actual* logic bend to *my* version of logic.

Do you know how empowering that has been for me... to be not just understood, but accepted with all my weirdness? No wonder I married a man so much like Daddyo in that way.

He patiently explained football to me when I was just shy of becoming a teenager, week after week, even though I often asked the strangest questions every Sunday. We'd eat pork rinds, fried onions, and leftover meatloaf sandwiches on Home Pride wheat bread with Miracle Whip, sitting in the basement, watching teams we barely cared about. We lived in Nebraska had no team but followed two sacred ABC rules on who to root for:

1. **Always Browns from Cleveland** *(Daddyo is from Youngstown, Ohio)*

2. **Anybody But Cowboys** *(well, duh)*.

I was mostly there for the snacks and the cute uniforms. And to have Daddyo all to myself on Sundays.

> **ME:** *"Wait... The guy who tackled the guy who caught the ball - isn't he basically playing the same position, but on defense?"*
>
> **DADDYO:** *"Sort of, baby. On defense, he's stopping the receiver. On offense, he IS the receiver."*
>
> **ME:** *"Got it. I'm going for the Dolphins. Those shiny blue pants? Adorable."*

DADDYO: *"Ok baby, that's fine. Anybody but the Cowboys is just fine by me."*

Back to the hernias. During my recovery, we put together puzzles we found in the hospital guest area. That turned into a tradition we kept going at home, long after I healed and to this day. While the rest of the world slept, we stayed up until 3 a.m., one of us working the border, the other tackling a complex pattern in the middle.

The puzzle wasn't the point. It was the conversation. The quiet companionship and comfortable silence. It's when he gave gentle advice about everything from boys to bullies.

When I went through the 4th, or was it the 5th, breakup with my high school boyfriend, Daddyo always knew what to say...

- *"You can't be with someone just because they want to be with you. They have to deserve you and bring out the best in you."*

- *"You only have one chance to have a first time, baby. Make sure he's worth your gift."*

- *"You can do bad by yourself, you don't need someone else making you feel this way."*

And then, there was the music. Oooh, the music! Daddyo taught me to hear harmony.

DADDYO: *"Listen to how Boléro builds - one instrument at a time. It becomes a masterpiece."*

ME: *"This is Prince. He sings all the parts, plays all the instruments, and harmonizes with himself. He IS the masterpiece."*

DADDYO: *"Okay baby, this here is The Persuasions - acapella harmony. I'll play this song twice. The second time, focus on a different voice."*

And just like that, I understood harmony. Can't sing it- ask anyone who has heard me do karaoke. Yikes.

I also understood six words I'll never forget.

When I was 16, I got drunk for the first time. Didn't even *know* I was drinking- I was the designated driver for crying out loud- WHY would *anyone* give the driver alcohol??

It was 1986 on a Saturday night in the teen party mecca of Omaha Nebraska. Someone handed me a fruity cup of punch at a party and said, "No alcohol in it!" (It came from a trash can. That should've been my first clue of that bald face lie.) I drank. A LOT. I danced. A LOT. I blacked out. I won a wet t-shirt contest.

Next thing I knew, I was on my deposited on my front porch with my friends burning rubber after banging on my front door. My mom opened the door and looked down at a puddle of Renee.

Mom: *"What's wrong with you?"*

ME (groaning): *"CRAMPS!"*

She sighed, handed me Motrin as I crawled across the kitchen and went back to bed. I made it to the basement couch before passing all the way out.

The next morning, I was jolted into consciousness by a gawdawful stench - Daddyo holding a glass of Old Grand-Dad bourbon under my nose.

ME: *"UGHHHHH!!!"*

As I booked to the bathroom and called dinosaurs... what in God's name smells like rancid peaches?!? Called more dinosaurs. I swear they called BACK. I crawled back to the couch without a shred of dignity.

DADDYO (cool as ever, uttered the six words that stayed with me until I was stationed in Germany in 1990):

"That's why YOU shouldn't drink, baby."

I rarely got drunk in high school after that - not just because I hated puking, but because I never wanted to let him down again. And to this day, I still cannot even SMELL peach schnapps.

Refill & Reflect

POURsonality Trait:

My Daddyo is Cab Franc.

A strong but humble powerhouse. Never flashy, but always memorable. He doesn't just blend - he *teaches* other varietals how to blend and still maintain their own identity.

He's the backbone in the background of Bordeaux. The parent of Merlot, Cabernet Sauvignon, and Carménère. He brings depth, structure, and harmony to every bottle - and every moment.

Sip Tip:

Look to Northern Virginia and California for Cab Francs that can be both barbecue casual and Beef Wellington fancy.

- Try Bozzo Family Vineyards. Their Cab Franc is smooth yet powerful and pairs with puzzle nights, acapella harmonies, and unconditional love.

- Cab Franc is more often the back up singer than the lead vocal in French and Italian blends, but it's often identifiable by a distinct green pepper characteristic that's quite nice with the right dish!

Share Your POUR Choice Story

Journal about who's your daddy.

_____
_____
_____
_____
_____
_____
_____
_____
_____
_____
_____
_____
_____
_____
_____
_____
_____
_____
_____
_____

Time To Wine About It!

Which wine pairs with your story: _____

Chapter 13
Paws On My Heart

In 2025, I woke up each morning hoping and praying that he would do the same. I would stare at him for 30 seconds, waiting to see his chest heave or watch his legs chase that dream rabbit.

While I know intellectually that he will cross that rainbow bridge someday- there's always the hope that today is NOT that day.

For 19 years, our Jack Russell, Beemer Marsalis Ventrice, has brought joy, laughter and comfort to our lives. Sure he farts when he stretches, he snores like a bear with a sinus infection, and his breath reeks of trout no matter WHAT he eats. But I wouldn't trade that for all the sweet smelling silence on earth.

He is our li'l Beemie boy, and he's the best prank Don and I ever pulled off.

When our son, Gino, was turning 8 years old in 2006, he wanted a "Jake Russell dog". Don resisted at first.

> **DON:** *"He's too young to walk a dog by himself, and we'll be the ones doing all the work."*

ME: *"You're right babe. We should wait. I mean, we'll still be taking care of it long after he graduates high school if we wait, but still, I think you're right."*

DON: *"On the other hand, if we get a dog now, by the time he graduates and leaves home, the dog will probably be on its way out too, then we can travel and have a fully empty nest… we should get a dog NOW."*

ME: *"That's brilliant babe, I think you're right. Let's get a dog."*

Did I know Jack Russells could live into their 20s? Yes. Did I tell Don this? ABSOLUTELY not. I wanted a dog too, and after all, it was Don's idea, right? Riiiiight.

Punk'd was a popular show at the time, and since "Extra" is my toxic trait, I set a double Punk in motion. While Don went in search of the perfect "Jake Russell", I pulled Gino aside.

ME: *"Hey Gino Bambino, Dad thinks you're too young for a dog, but why don't we trick him into thinking I got you a real dog, but it's really a stuffed animal!"*

Gino (practicing tae kwon do sparring moves): "Yeah yeah yeah! Like a build-a-bear ® but it's a dog! HiiiiYAH!"

That's my boy, he already knew how to pull this off. What he didn't know is that the "Build a Puppy website" was a three page Word document, and that the prompts were leading him to build Beemer, since Don had already picked him out of the litter and I knew what he looked like.

We thought of everything, down to the letter Gino received a few days later certifying that his 'Jake Russell' named Beemer would be delivered in a green dog carrier.

The big day came, after his bowling birthday party his best friend came back to the house with his father to hang out for awhile. Don was "called away to work" so Gino had some time to practice his "I got a dog" speech while we waited for the special delivery.

Don returned home as Gino the jumping bean practiced endless Tae Kwon Do spinning back kicks fueled by birthday cake and gummy worms.

DON (opening the door): *"I'm hooome! Heyyy, there a green bag on the porch...'*

GINO (sprinting for the door): *"That's MIIIINE!"*

He grabs the carrier from Don, we cringe as he whips it around and carries it to the living room where he plops it down and tells Don to have a seat.

GINO (hands innocently behind his back): *"Daddy, I know you said I was too young for a dog but mommy said I could have one and I promise to walk it and feed it and pick up its poop and too bad Dad, MOMMY SAID."*

He kneels down to unzip the carrier and... it moved! Gino jumped back.

GINO: *"What the..."*

GINO'S BUDDY: *"Is it a robot dog??"*

GINO'S BUDDY'S DAD (who is in on it): *"Quiet son!"*

Gingerly, Gino reaches out to finish unzipping the carrier, and out pops 10 week old, fuzzy 4lbs of Beemer!

Gino freezes- his brain confused as to why his stuffed dog is MOVING.

DON AND ME: *"YOU GOT PUNK'D! HAPPY BIRTHDAY!"*

G was still in shock as Beemer crawled right into his lap. Thanks to Gino's blanket that we tucked into the carrier, Beemer immediately recognized that funky little boy smell.

Beemer has been nothing but joy ever since that day, his life could be a book of his own. Hmmm... The POURky Little puppy...ok that title needs work.

He's given us a few scares over the years... he ate a bee just a few days after we brought him home and his whole face puffed up like a cartoon. Fun fact: the $300 Benadryl vet bill wasn't funny.

He killed Peter Rabbit on Easter Sunday, but that wasn't his fault. A bunny literally jumped into his mouth when he was just a few months old!

Unfortunately for that rabbit, it was the same day Beemer got his first squeak toy. Not so fun fact: when you squeeze a real bunny, it sounds JUST like a squeak toy... the rest of the story tells itself.

He cornered opossum and groundhogs twice his size, brought us live snapping turtles and dead digging voles that dared to venture into his backyard.

He learned ten tricks in a row- all you had to do was hold a jerky treat above his head and the show would begin: spin, lay down, roll over, play dead, army crawl, circle mommy, weave between legs, sit, give paw, sit pretty!

He's been our happy little shadow for almost 20 years. Through surgeries and sickness he wouldn't leave our sides, even if he heard the crinkle of a cheese wrapper.

When we came through the door, he'd gallop around the corner with a ball or toy in tow, ready to play. He protected our home from everything- raccoons, foxes, skittering leaves- if it moved outside, he let us know.

Now when we come home, we have to nudge him awake. He's still a watch dog, except now he just watches the world go by. And when you hold up a treat, he just shakes his little back legs and stares:

BEEMER: *"I'm 88 years old lady, the shows over. Just gimme the damn treat!"*

And we still feel the same joy every time.

Just like us, he's slower, his joints pop, he takes medicine for everything from arthritis to reflux. But that pokey little puppy still shines in his mostly blind eyes.

He might not hear the door open and close anymore, but he still comes cruising around the corner when that cheese wrapper crinkles.

Who's a good boy? Beemer is.

Refill & Reflect

POURsonality Trait:

Beemer is a blend of every memorable moment, whether mundane or marvelous.

He's popcorn with Chardonnay and Netflix, home alone.

He's sushi with Riesling at your favorite restaurant with friends.

He's homemade sauce and pasta with Chianti for Sunday dinner with family.

He's dark chocolate and sea salt covered strawberries with Cabernet Franc with the one you love.

Like wine, no matter what the occasion, he's the perfect pairing. He was still alive and kicking when I finished this book, and will live forever through the tattoos of his paws on each of us, and the decades of memories his paws have left on our hearts. Diamonds aren't *this* girl's best friend- jerky treats are.

Sip Tip:

Cherish your mutt's mundane moments as much as your marvelous memories. That's it. That's the tip.

Share Your POUR Choice Story

Journal about the paw marks on your heart.

_____
_____
_____
_____
_____
_____
_____
_____
_____
_____
_____
_____
_____
_____
_____
_____
_____
_____
_____
_____
_____
_____

Time To Wine About It!

Which wine pairs with your story: _____

Chapter 14
Raising a Chardonnay Kid in a Pinot Noir World

Turns out, being a parent is a lot like planting a vineyard.

You either raise a basic, two-buck chuck that sits at eye level in the grocery store…

or you cultivate a fine vintage - complex, rare, and worthy of cellaring.

Let's talk about why I wanted my kid to be a lot like **Chardonnay.** Chardonnay is resilient.

It can thrive in almost any climate.

It adapts, bends, survives.

It can be buttery or crisp, oaked or stainless, still or sparkling, yet it *never* loses its core characteristics. And the best part?

Chardonnay doesn't care if you love it or not. It knows its value and unapologetically has no f**ks to give which version of it you hate.

Now, the *world* my Chardonnay was born into?

Pure Pinot Noir.

Now, Pinot Noir can be legendary, sure. But it's also sensitive.

Thin-skinned. Moody.

The world today can be all of that, we often politically correct ourselves to keep the peace instead of creating controversy. That's not all bad, but like growing great Pinot Noir... it can be exhausting.

It needs damn near *perfect* weather, *ideal* soil composition, and just the right amount of sun, shade and slope to become great. You can't accidentally grow an excellent Pinot Noir, you have to know your stuff in the vineyard.

In other words: not our kid. We had no clue what we were doing, so we raised him to split the sidewalk on his own like a tree root. But not just that - he knows how to play nice with Pinot Noir and others - remember that Chardonnay adaptability...? He's got it. So far, so good...

REFILL & REFLECT

POURSONALITY TRAIT:

Oh, my darling Pinot Noir...

You're not for beginners! You definitely aren't an easy one. But damn, you sure are worth the effort!

And Chardonnay, thank you so much for being so flexible and easy to hang around. You make Pinot Noir less of a pain in the ass!

Sip Tip:

Pinot Noir, you are complex, delicate, and not always in the mood to be understood. You're not meant to impress everyone, only those who truly understand your journey and appreciate your gifts.

- Don't chase the most expensive label- chase the one that feels like a story worth sipping. Go beyond Burgundy and explore Pinot Noir from Oregon, Washington and Sonoma.

- Let it breathe. Pinot reveals itself slowly, like a guarded friend who needs a little time. You'll love what happens as it opens up and shares its secrets.

- Pair it with something unexpected- salmon, mushrooms, or your next deep conversation.

Chardonnay is your exact opposite and yet your closest friend, and affects people the same way - just without the temper tantrums. I already gave you Sip Tips on Chardonnay, but here's one more:

- NEVER turn down the chance to try one from a new region. It can grow in almost any climate, so it has the POURsonality range of Jamie Foxx and Meryl Streep. Comedy, drama- Chardonnay can play any role!

Share Your POUR Choice Story

Journal about what you're glad you worked hard for.

_____
_____
_____
_____
_____
_____
_____
_____
_____
_____
_____
_____
_____
_____
_____
_____
_____
_____
_____
_____

Time To Wine About It!

Which wine pairs with your story: _____

Chapter 15

From Planted to Priceless

Wine tasting is like meeting someone new. At first, you notice how they look, how they smell, how they make you feel. But first impressions are limited.

You're only getting a glimpse of who that person is today. You're not seeing all the hard work, heartbreak, love & life experiences that made them who they are, or how they will develop for years to come.

It mirrors the years of careful preparation, dedication and nurturing that go into a vineyard & all the patience it takes for that delicious wine to make its way into your glass.

That first sip can tell you a lot, but it doesn't tell you the whole story. So let me serve you a full pour of what it takes to raise a fine vintage and grow a great human...

Stage 1: Dormancy (Pregnancy)

In vineyards, dormancy is when the vines rest. Doesn't sound like much, right? But they aren't *just resting*.

The vines are actually storing energy deep in their roots to prepare themselves for the sacred process of bearing fruit - but nothing is visible above ground.

Pregnancy happens the same way - all the important work is happening deep beneath the surface and away from prying eyes.

I was one of those hated women who had a *phenomenal* pregnancy.

Glowing skin, thick hair, still teaching fitness classes until ten days before giving birth.

People barely knew I was pregnant unless I turned sideways. (Well, except for the nose. That thing spread like it was renting out space.)

> **DON:** *"NeNe, it looks like you're carrying the baby in your nose, not your stomach."*
>
> **ME:** *"One more crack like that and you'll be carrying my foot in your ass. Go get me a Big Mac and two waffles to atone."*

We did it the old-school way: Bradley Method, no drugs, deep breathing, lots of "you got this, NeNe" from Don.

Then, after two and a half hours of labor (yes, I said *hours*, not days), I was blissfully napping my way through it until they woke me up to push.

Don was like Yogi Berra behind the plate, and caught six pounds, eleven ounces of perfect, squirmy, wailing glory.

His name is Gino. And he was born with purpose. He was the piece that made our family puzzle complete.

Just like planting the right grape in the right place, at the right time, we gave him everything he needed: a loving home- we didn't have much as an enlisted military family, but we made it work. The nutrients to grow, but not in a fanatical way that made him vomit if he smelled a Dorito. He ingested just enough junk to build immunity.

And most importantly, exposure to struggle so he'd become resilient. The first two he could control when he matured, but the struggle is what created strength as his default. Don and I know firsthand because we were both planted to grow the same way.

Yes, 1998 was a *very* good year, the Yankees won the world series, my nose returned to its original size, and we crushed our first and only vintage.

Stage 2: Bud Break (Infancy)

This is when tiny buds appear and shoots start to grow. It's the start of the visible journey.

Fun fact: I didn't think I'd be a great mom.

I had only voluntarily held ONE baby before Gino in my whole life! I didn't melt at baby gurgles or think it was cute when they farted. I wasn't one of those people who saw a baby and immediately started "cooing" and making silly faces. It actually annoyed me... when a fully grown adult would see a baby and all of a sudden start speaking goo-goo-ga-ga gibberish in this high pitched tone that was completely unnecessary, then acted like they just couldn't help themselves.

Uggh - I just didn't get it! My maternal instinct was basically: "He better be able to kill spiders when he's older."

But... we had a parenting plan.

We refused to spoil him or make baby talk.

He was fed, clothed, safe, and loved. But we had to let him cry it out, even as it broke our hearts. We taught him that comfort can come from within, and that self-soothing was a super power.

And that's what bud break is about, believe it or not. The vines thrust themselves deep into rocky soil to find nutritious minerals. They lean into the sun for photosynthesis, and learn how to get what they need to grow & survive on their own, without constant hand-holding and begin to flower.

Weak vines and spoiled brats are the result of too much pampering, and will produce unremarkable grapes and needy children.

But if you want the good stuff... that comes from a little friction and a lotta grit.

Stage 3: Flowering (Toddlerhood)

Flowering is a very delicate period when the tiny grape flowers bloom, self-pollinate, and begin their journey towards becoming fruit. It needs the right environment. Weather matters.

Too cold, too wet, too windy for too long - and the crop could fail. But the vines have to figure it out on their own.

Letting Gino eat dirt might have been controversial.

Yes, you read that right.

Little toddler Gino would sit in the front yard, face to the sun, cool grass in one drool-covered hand, sun-baked mud coating the other. I watched him curiously lift a drooly dirt-caked finger to his mouth...

Other moms might yell, "Nooo, that's yucky!"

Me?

Nah, I let him do it.

He gagged. Spit. Never did it again. Why leave him curious about eating dirt? Let him decide not to on his own.

The best life lessons come from experiences, not restrictions. Sometimes, when we interfere to protect the people we love, we rob them of the opportunity to grow and to, someday, regale others with a cool dinner party story.

That's what flowering is. Trust nature to take its course. Let the vines find their way.

You may need to do some pruning, guide them to grow in the right direction, but ultimately:

LET. THEM. EAT. DIRT.

Stage 4: Fruit Set (Puberty begins)

During fruit set, the flowers that became small, hard green balls will soon blossom into full fledged grapes. Yup, it's grape puberty. And let me tell you - fruit set hit HARD in our little vineyard.

At age 9, we were baby grape Gino's heroes.

By age 10? He had toe hair and opinions. Lots of them.

GINO: *"Mom! I've got puberty on my toes!"*

ME: *"Wait... what did you spill on your toes? Wipe it up!"*

GINO (foot in my face): *"No! Look! PUBERTY!"*

He started challenging everything. Bedtime. Logic. Authority.

GINO: *"Why do I have to go to bed now?"*

ME: *"Because you need your rest so you can pay attention in school tomorrow."*

GINO: *"Why don't you have to go to bed? Don't you have to pay attention at work?"*

ME: *"Yes, but I'm a grown up and I don't need as much sleep as a child, my dear."*

GINO: *"That doesn't make sense. You always say you're tired, but I'M not tired, so I must not need as much rest as you think. Maybe YOU need more sleep and I need less sleep."*

ME: *"What I'm really tired of right now is this conversation. Gino, now please go get ready for bed!"*

GINO: *"If you're THAT tired maybe you should go to bed too..."*

It was frustrating. Exhausting. But also... it was exactly what we wanted.

He learned to think critically. Push back. Trust, but verify.

We were raising a grape with backbone.

Stage 5: Veraison (the end of childhood)

As the grapes continue their journey to becoming wine, they begin to morph into their true colors and flavors through a transformational process called veraison. In the vineyard, veraison lasts a few months, but in our home- it lasted six long, stressful years.

Gino's focus shifted from what mom and dad could do for him to what he could do for himself. He wasn't a vulnerable flower anymore, he could think for himself and started making decisions.

> **GINO (at ten years old)**: *"MOM. I'm getting too old for hugs and kisses good night- that's for babies. I'm practically a man now"* - he said seriously, while wiggling his newly hairy toes.
>
> **ME (hiding the tiny piece of my heart that just shattered)**: *"Hmm, ok, if that's how you feel, I respect that. What if we make a fist bump our kiss good night, and paper-covers-rock can be a hug?"*
>
> **GINO**: *"Whatever, yeah, sure, that's fine."*

Veraison is like the end of puberty, without the rebellion and backtalk. It's beautiful to witness in a vineyard, the grapes morphing through various colors, as delightful to witness as changing leaves in autumn.

But in a home, its beauty usually isn't appreciated until long after the harvest. In fact, while the change is happening, you're tempted to pull those vines out by their roots and send them to military school. By the grace of **Dionysus***, we made it through.

We had two simple rules:

1) every action was followed by a reaction. When you do the right thing, you're rewarded. When you do the wrong thing, there are consequences. We made it clear what each reaction would be, and allowed him to choose his action.

2) DFU which stands for: Don't Fuck Up. See rule 1 for clarity.

Gino's veraison years were literally and figuratively shaped by baseball. From being born during the World Series, to being a star player the game from kindergarten through high school- life was baseball and baseball was life.

Strike Out: doing the wrong thing, getting caught and sent back to the dugout.

> **DON**: "You're grounded Gino- you chose to break the rule, so you chose consequence.

Double: not just doing the right thing, going the extra mile

> **ME**: "Thank you for doing your chores and two of mine! We'll extend your curfew by an hour, go have fun tonight, DFU!"

Balk: lying or not doing what you promised.

> **ME**: "I forgot is not an excuse G- tell your friends you won't be accessible for the next few days and hand over your phone."

Walk: getting a pass instead of a consequence.

> **DON**: "We're giving you a break this time because you got all As on your report card but DFU again."

Can we just pause a sec and be annoyed that balk and walk aren't pronounced the same...? English is MESSY.

Beyond those analogies, baseball raised us as a family. It's a game of failure, where doing your job well 50% of the time at the plate gets you into the hall of fame.

The measure of greatness isn't how many home runs you hit, it's in how consistently you support your team with RBIs, how well you recover from making an error, and how strongly you lead after a loss.

Those veraison years handed us walk off home runs and championship wins along with devastating losses and character testing moments that threatened to destroy the entire crop. But Gino weathered every storm, and produced hearty, quality clusters that were ready to leave the vineyard right on time.

Stage 6: Harvest (College)

And then, suddenly… it was time.

Move-in day. Dorm drop-off.

The vineyard had done its job. The grapes were ripe.

Now it was Gino's job to become the winemaker of his own life.

> **DON (hugging Gino):** *"We're proud of you. Never forget: your word is your bond. Don't make choices for temporary pleasure that end up with permanent consequences."*

GINO: *"I'll be the man you raised, Dad. I won't let you or myself down."*

ME (hugging him tightly but quickly): *"There are three A's you can't get in college: Arrested, Addicted, and A Baby. Got it?"*

GINO (laughing): *"Yes, Mama. I got it."*

I patted his handsome cheek and turned to walk away.

GINO: *"Mom?"*

ME: *"Yes, son?"*

I turned around to see him reach out his fist...

We bumped. Paper covered rock, holding each "hug" a little longer than usual. I smiled so hard it hurt.

Then he pulled me into a real hug "Thank you for everything Mama"... and I *lost it*. But I knew, in that moment, he was going to be GRAPE. I mean - he was going to be GREAT. (*They're the same thing to me...*)

We harvested a vintage that's still aging, still deepening in complexity.

He was 26 as of the day I wrote this book. And he's not just a wine in my glass like the others - he's the **region of Champagne.**

Why?

Because most Champagne requires both Pinot Noir and Chardonnay to exist at its best.

Because he developed well under pressure.

Because he's rare, respected, and only gets better with time.

And because he came from a home that wasn't always easy on him, and thrived because of all the messy, beautiful moments along the way.

Refill & Reflect

POURsonality Trait:

We may manage the vineyard, but the grapes make the wine. Champagne has to do a lot on its own to be excellent - we are just the guides on its journey.

Our job is to give them good - not great - soil, so they learn to find greatness, not feel entitled to it. To let deep roots develop, so they can become strong and independent.

Most of all, we provide an environment that nurtures them - not to become what we want them to be - to become what they were always meant to be.

Sip Tip:

Champagne is typically a combination of Chardonnay, Pinot Noir and Pinot Muniere: three very different grapes that come together to create a superior wine.

- If you want a champagne made of only white varietals, look for Blanc de Blanc on the label. It could have other white grapes in addition to Chardonnay.

- If you want only red grapes in your bubbles, look for Blanc de Noir - it's 100% Pinot Noir.

- If you want to experience the best of both worlds, pop a bottle without preconceived notions and let the traditional blend impress you!

PS: Spectacular sparkling wine doesn't HAVE to be Champagne. Cava from Spain is a delightful wallet-friendly sparkler that is a must try! If you get to Virginia- grab a bottle of Breauxmance from Breaux Vineyards.

Both of these fine wines are made in the same traditional method as champagne- stretch your palate and taste these three side-by-side-by-side! Your tastebuds will thank you.

Share Your POUR Choice Story

Journal about nurturing your best vintage.

_____
_____
_____
_____
_____
_____
_____
_____
_____
_____
_____
_____
_____
_____
_____
_____
_____
_____
_____
_____

Time To Wine About It!

Which wine pairs with your story: _____

Renee's Terms & Definitions
Glossary

Slap the bag: Apparently you remove the bag from the boxed wine, and slap it to nudge the remnants from the bottom to empty the bag. Never done it personally- you can thank Gino for sharing the first thing he learned in college at West Virginia University with me, and now- all of you.

Don't Serve Me Broccoli and Tell Me it's Greens: An African American saying, meaning don't give me a cubic zirconia and tell me it's a diamond. Listen to the song by Arrested Development- you'll love what you learn.

Bizlationships®: My trademarked business coaching strategy for developing mutually beneficial connections through organic conversations. I love a good mash up, can't believe this one didn't already exist!

DTR talks: "Define The Relationship" talks. Clearly my editor is WAY younger than me- I had to look that shit up too.

Porch Pounder: Although I introduce this term under the Booty Call chapter, it's not sexual, well, not at FIRST. It refers to a wine that you can crush from beginning to end while watching the world go by from your porch. Any additional pounding is optional. And highly recommended.

WineauxClock®: It's the time you drink wine, the year you open the bottle, the moment you discover a new love by the glass. It's also front and center in a future POUR series book... but don't tell anyone, it's a surprise for the rest of the world.

Cosplay: The practice of dressing up as a character from a movie, book, or video game.

Gatekeep: The act of controlling, and usually limiting, access to something.

Dionysus: The Greek god of wine, winemaking, fertility, theatre, religious ecstasy, and madness. No, he wasn't in the Blinded by the Light chapter - *but oooh how i wish he was...*

Davy Jones Locker: the bottom of the sea, especially regarded as the grave of sailors drowned at sea.

About The Author
Meet Renee...

When Renee was 8 years old, she flew face first onto hot, summer asphalt while failing miserably at learning to ride a bike. She didn't know it then, but this experience of a mouthful of hot rocks and melted tar, mixed with grass clippings and dandelions, would shape her palate's recognition of the non-food factors in wine, and her appreciation for savoring the flavor of life experiences.

A US Navy veteran turned wine whisperer, serial entrepreneur, and bestselling author, Renee believes that life and business are best enjoyed with a good pour and great company.

She co-founded the award-winning Cork & Keg Tours in 2016, which she and her husband, Don, sold in 2023. Now, she leads WineauxClock® Culinary Experiences, blending wine education with life lessons.

Renee is also the creator of Bizlationships®, a methodology that transforms casual connections into revenue-generating professional relationships. Her debut book, POUR Relationship Choices, uncorks the parallels between wine and the relationships we nurture... good, bad, and beautiful.

When she's not hosting wine events or speaking at industry conferences, Renee shares her insights on the "Start Wine-ing" podcast. She's been featured in United Airlines Hemispheres magazine and has guest-hosted the James Beard Taste Award-winning show, *V is for Vino*.

Renee's mission is to help professionals and entrepreneurs create meaningful connections that pour into their personal and professional lives.

She and Don, her husband of over 30 years, live in Loudoun County Virginia with their 19 year old Jack Russell, Beemer, and have a 26 year old son, Gino.

While she STILL cannot ride a bike, she CAN drive a conversation about wine, life and experiences beyond the glass.

Learn more at reneeventrice.com.